Please note: the brief introductions to each section and to the book as a whole are designed for adults to read. Children can happily play with the book on their own but will also gain a great deal from adult participation. The introductions explain how and why adults can help children to learn through playing.

First published 1984 by
The Hamlyn Publishing Group Limited
Michelin House, 81 Fulham Road, London SW3 6RB
Reprinted 1985, 1989
© **Copyright The Hamlyn Publishing Group Limited 1984**
ISBN 0 600 38929 4
Printed in Italy
Some of the illustrations and stories in this book have
previously appeared in other books published by The Hamlyn
Publishing Group Limited.

Acknowledgements
World's Work Ltd. and Doubleday & Company, Inc., for 'What is
Red?' from *Hailstones and Halibut Bones* **by Mary O'Neill**
(copyright © 1961 by Mary Le Duc O'Neill).

PLAYTIME LEARNING

Compilation: Janet Slingsby
Educational Consultant: Henry Pluckrose

HAMLYN

Introduction

From the moment of birth children begin to learn. Indeed, the years children spend at home, before they go to school, are perhaps the most significant years of their lives. During this period, children learn to walk and to talk and so begin to discover the nature of the world into which they have been born.

For children to learn effectively, they need help. Nowhere is this more obvious than in language. By listening to words, repeating words, and then by using words to convey an idea, children master speech. They learn through experience, experience gained in most part from the adults in their lives.

This book provides a way of extending that experience. It sets out, quite simply, to help adults and children to share the fun and enjoyment of learning. In it, topics like numbers, colours, shapes, the seasons and the human body, are introduced in such a way that the child's understanding is extended. The simple questions, which are central to the text, provide the opportunity for children to talk and so to question more.

For the toddler this is a book to look at and to talk about. Older children, approaching school age, may find that they can 'read' some of the pages themselves. This early 'reading' will probably be from memory. Listen when children 'read' in this way. They are imitating the ability you have to give meaning to marks on paper. Later they will be able to interpret these marks (or words) whenever they occur. By encouraging children in this way you will show that you are interested in their developing skills. Modern research has shown that when parents devote time to their children, performance in the classroom is much more likely to be successful.

This book also contains a number of games, puzzles and activities. Some of these are too difficult for the young child to attempt unaided. Their purpose is to encourage adults and children to 'play' together. So try to find time to make things with your children and to play games with them. The early years of life are a time when so much is learned from the adults with whom a child is growing up. It is a time of sharing.

Henry Pluckrose

Contents

Colours

Some children seem to learn which colour is which overnight. Other children confuse red and yellow for months! As with all attempts to 'teach' young children, it is very important not to make a great deal of fuss about the speed at which they learn or how well they retain information. Putting pressure on a child is a sure way of stopping them learning altogether because learning new things ceases to be fun.

In fact there is no need to make children aware that you are 'teaching' them the names of colours at all. Point out the colours of their clothes when they are getting dressed: 'Here is your red jumper.' 'Do you want your blue shoes or your yellow wellingtons?'

When you go out for walks, or just out shopping, have a 'pink' walk or a 'red' walk and see who can spot the most pink or red objects. You can play this game on car journeys too. Older children who already know their colours will still enjoy a competition like this.

Red

This rose is red. The cherries and the tomato are red too. Do you like eating cherries? Be careful not to swallow the stones! Are tomatoes always red?

What is red?

Red is a sunset
Blazing and bright.
Red is feeling brave
With all your might.
Red is a sunburn
Spot on your nose.
Sometimes red
Is a red, red rose.
Red squiggles out
When you cut your hand.
Red is a brick and
The sound of a band.
Red is a hotness
You get inside
When you're embarrassed
And want to hide.
Firecracker, fire-engine
Fire-flicker red —

And when you're angry
Red runs through your head.
Red is an Indian,
A valentine heart,
The trimming on
A circus cart.
Red is a lipstick,
Red is a shout,
Red is a signal
That says: 'Watch out!'
Red is a great big
Rubber ball.
Red is the giant-est
Colour of all.
Red is a show-off
No doubt about it —
But can you imagine
Living without it?

Mary O'Neill

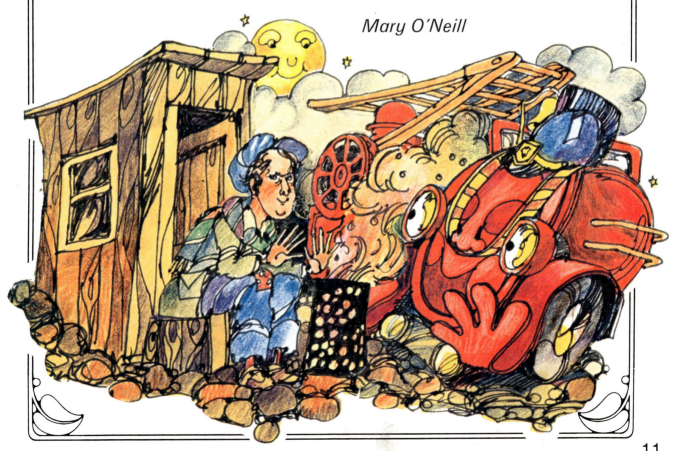

The red coat

One morning Susan and her Mummy were going shopping. Susan's Mummy opened the cupboard and took out her coat.

'Why don't you wear this pretty red coat?' asked Susan, pointing to it.

Mummy laughed. 'It is too small for me now,' she said. 'I will have to give it to a jumble sale.'

'But it is such a nice colour,' said Susan. 'Red is my favourite colour.'

Susan's Mummy looked at the coat. 'Do you know, Susan,' she said, 'I've had an idea. I think I could use this coat to make a dressing-gown for you. You need a new one.'

'Ooh, yes please,' said Susan.

That afternoon Susan's Mummy was very busy snipping and stitching and using the sewing-machine.

Susan watched her making the little velvet collar and cuffs. Mummy gave her the little bits of velvet that were left over. Susan liked the feel of them. They were rather like fur.

At last Mummy said, 'Nearly finished now — just the buttons to put on.'

That night Susan *wanted* bedtime to come! She had her bath early and then she put on her lovely new dressing-gown. She counted the buttons as she did them up: one, two, three, four, five, six, seven, eight!

When she went downstairs Daddy said, 'Hello, little Robin Redbreast! That *is* a lovely dressing-gown.'

Susan climbed on to his knee to hear her bedtime story. The red dressing-gown kept her snug and warm.

Yellow

Bananas are yellow. So are baby chicks. How many baby chicks can you see? Do you know what these chicks will be when they grow up? They will be hens and lay eggs for your breakfast.

This little boy is called Tom. He likes the rain. Tom is wearing a hat and a raincoat. What colour is Tom's raincoat?

Three ducks are following Tom. See if you can count the ducks — one, two, three.

Tom is splashing in the puddles. Do you walk in puddles? Tom's feet won't get wet because he is wearing wellington boots.

Blue

Look at this big blue fish. He is playing in the sea. Have you ever been to the seaside? Is the sea always blue?

This little girl is called Lucy. Lucy has got a very special pet. He is a mynah bird called Sam. Sam can talk. He can say, 'Hello Lucy' and 'Goodbye Lucy'.

Sam looks out of the window every afternoon to see if Lucy is coming home from school. As soon as she turns the corner he calls out, 'Hello Lucy'.

Today Lucy took Sam to a pet show. Her big sister told her that if Sam won first prize he would have a blue ribbon hung around his neck. If he won second prize he would have a red ribbon. If he won third prize he would have a yellow ribbon.

Which prize did Sam win?

The blue handkerchief

Christopher was going to school. His Mummy said, 'Take this new handkerchief with you,' and she gave him a bright blue one.

Christopher ran to catch the school bus. As he ran, the handkerchief dropped out of his pocket.

A man came walking along. 'What's this!' he said. He picked up the blue handkerchief.

'Just what I need for the sun, today!' he said, and he tied a knot in each corner. Then he put the handkerchief on his head, and went off to work in the fields.

But a gust of wind blew the handkerchief off his head. A lady with her shopping on a bicycle came along. She was trying hard to ride with a broken seat. She saw the blue handkerchief.

'Just what I need!' she cried. She tied the seat up with it, and happily pedalled home.

At home, her little boy was crying. 'My kite won't fly!' he sobbed.

'Why,' she said, 'it won't fly because you have lost its tail.'

She took the handkerchief off her bicycle, and tied it to the kite. Up it soared, high into the air, the piece of bright blue flapping in the wind. But after a while, the wind pulled too hard at the handkerchief, and tugged it off.

A little boy found it and used it to wrap up his collection of stones.

Later on, he bumped into Christopher. 'Look at my stones, Christopher!' he said, and took the blue handkerchief full of stones out of his pocket.

Christopher stared. 'That's my handkerchief!' he said.

'Is it really?' said the boy. 'Well you had better have it back, then!'

Later on, Christopher's Mummy saw the blue handkerchief.

'How on earth has it got into such a terrible state?' cried Mummy.

But Christopher couldn't answer. How was *he* to know?

Green

Can you see the big green caterpillar? He is sitting on a green leaf. Do you know what caterpillars turn into? Some turn into butterflies. Others turn into moths.

Green apples

Once there was an orchard full of apple trees. It was summertime and, as the sun shone, all the apples began to turn red. All except the apples on one tree. Those apples stayed green no matter how brightly the sun shone.

People came and started picking the red apples. Sometimes they stopped work and ate some of the red apples. But no one wanted to eat the green apples. The green apple tree was miserable and the red apple trees felt sorry for him.

Then one day the farmer and his wife came into the orchard. 'Those cooking apples look lovely,' said the farmer's wife. 'I think I will make a big apple pie on Sunday.'

'I'll tell the men to pick the cooking apples tomorrow,' said the farmer.

At last the green apple tree was happy. He realized that his apples were for cooking. Everyone knows that cooking apples never turn red!

Orange

Which do you like best — oranges or orange drinks? The orange drink is a fizzy one. Look at the bubbles! Can you count the bubbles in the drink? How many bubbles can you see floating above the drink?

Purple

Here is a big bunch of purple grapes. Some grapes are purple and some are green. Next time you go out shopping see if you can find some purple grapes and some green grapes.

Mixing colours

Have you got a paint-box? If you have, try mixing some red paint with some yellow paint. What colour do you get when you mix red and yellow?

What colour paint do you get if you mix blue and yellow paint?

What colour paint do you get if you mix red and blue paint?

Pink

This ice-cream is pink. Ice-cream comes in lots of different colours. How many different sorts have you tasted? Which is your favourite kind of ice-cream?

Emma has just had a bath. She has got a great big pink towel. Her Mummy gave it to her. Pink is Emma's favourite colour. She has got two pink dresses and some pink dungarees.

What colour are the clothes you are wearing today?

It is nearly Emma's bedtime. It is much too late for her to take the puppy for a walk. Never mind — tomorrow they will go to the park.

Brown

This brown bird is sitting on a brown branch. The bird is waiting to see if the children are going to put out any crumbs for him. Do you feed the birds? When you are next in the park look for a brown bird.

Black White Grey

The black rabbit has got floppy ears. The white rabbit has got a fluffy tail. The grey rabbit has got very long ears. All the rabbits have the same colour fur inside their ears. What colour is it?

Colour quiz

What colour is the grass?
Can you point to the yellow butterfly?
Where is the little red beetle?

Can you see the green and yellow butterfly?
How many pink flowers can you see?
Where is the purple flower?
What colour is the butterfly on the red flower?

The colourful clown

A picture that is black and white looks very different from a picture that is in colour. Why don't you draw a picture of a clown? Then you could colour him with your felt pens or crayons. Make sure he has a big red nose!

Numbers

When you use this book with young children, try to add a personal note with questions and games of your own. Extend the learning activities into everyday life. Count every time you walk up and down stairs with a child, or every time you do up their buttons. Ask the child to help by bringing you a certain number of items from another room.

Sing the rhymes even if you can't sing very well — the rhythm will help the child remember. As you sing, try to emphasize the number which the rhyme or story is illustrating. 'Dramatising' the rhyme using toys as characters can be fun, but just counting on your fingers or the child's fingers is a good substitute on busy days.

1 one

Hickory, dickory, dock!

Hickory, dickory, dock!
The mouse ran up the clock.
The clock struck one,
The mouse ran down,
Hickory, dickory, dock.

2 two

Two little blue birds

Two little blue birds
Sitting on a wall.
One named Peter,
One named Paul.

Fly away, Peter,
Fly away, Paul.
Come back, Peter,
Come back, Paul!

3 three

Three little kittens

Three little kittens,
They lost their mittens,
And they began to cry,
'O Mother dear,
We sadly fear,
That we have lost our mittens.'

'What! Lost your mittens,
You naughty kittens!
Then you shall have no pie.
Mee-ow, mee-ow,
Then you shall have no pie.'

The three little kittens,
They found their mittens,
And they began to cry,
'O Mother dear,
Come here, come here,
For we have found our mittens!'

'What! Found your mittens,
You good little kittens,
Then you shall have some pie.
Purr, purr, purr, purr,
Then you shall have some pie.'

The three little kittens
Put on their mittens,
And soon ate up their pie.
'O Mother dear, we greatly fear
That we have soiled our mittens.'

'What! Soiled your mittens,
You naughty kittens.'
And they began to cry,
'Mee-ow, mee-ow,'
And they began to cry.

The three little kittens,
They washed their mittens,
And hung them out to dry.
'O Mother dear, come here, come here,
For we have washed our mittens.'

'What! Washed your mittens?
You good little kittens.
Now hush, hush,
I smell a mouse close by,
I smell a mouse close by!'

4 four

The four children

Once upon a time there were four children. Sally was the eldest. Then came Michael, Paul and little Elizabeth. Daddy called them 'The Fearsome Four'!

One day the children were playing in the garden when Sally said, 'Let's pretend to be witches and wizards and make some magic.'

So Michael fetched a very large saucepan from the kitchen. Paul and Elizabeth collected lots of weeds and Sally stirred everything together with water from the pond.

They chanted lots of rhymes and spells but nothing happened. Then Mummy came out and was very cross with them for spoiling her saucepan! They were all sent to bed early.

But the four children were rather naughty. When it was dark they crept out into the garden to look for their witch's brew. Imagine their surprise when they found a real witch sitting beside it!

'Well, speak up!' she said crossly. 'Why did you call me here?'

The children were too scared to answer.

'I hope you are not wasting my time,' the witch said. 'I know a giant who is very fond of little children — to eat that is! Seeing as there are four of you I don't expect anyone would miss one.'

'We are the Fearsome *Four*!' said Sally bravely. She grabbed Elizabeth's hand and ran as fast as she could towards the house. Michael and Paul followed close behind.

In the morning only Sally remembered about the witch. Perhaps she had the adventure in her dreams. What do you think?

5 five

40

One, two, three, four, five

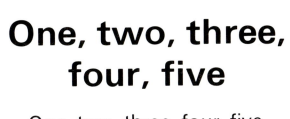

One, two, three, four, five,
Once I caught a fish alive.
Six, seven, eight, nine, ten,
Then I let it go again.

Why did you let it go?
Because it bit my finger so.
Which finger did it bite?
This little finger on the right.

6
six

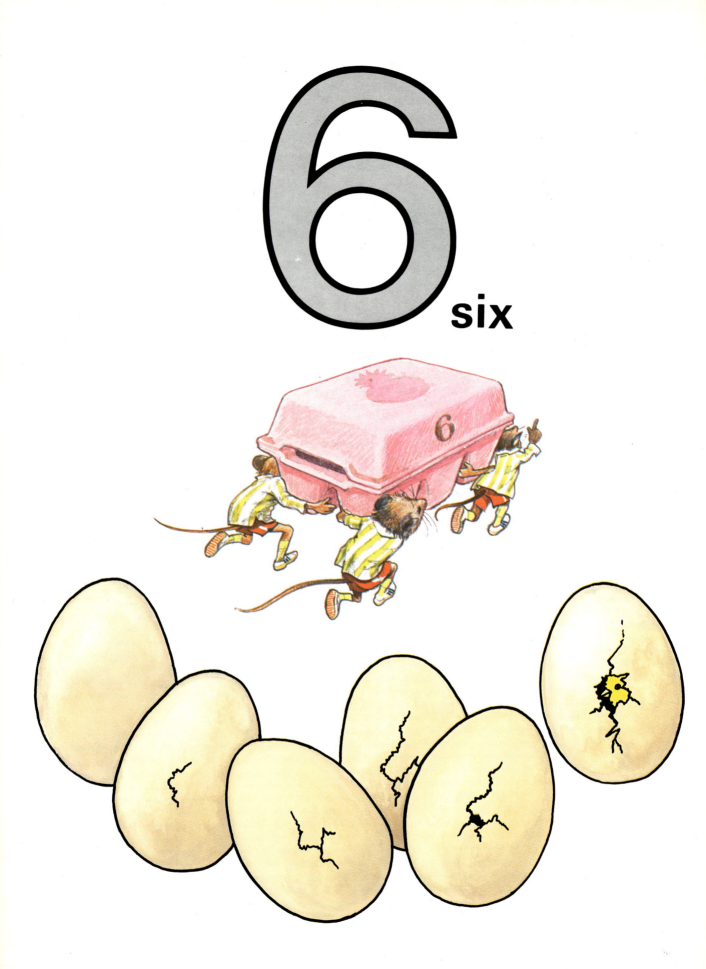

7
seven

8 eight

Peter is trying to catch a butterfly. How many butterflies can you see in the picture? There are eight butterflies. Three of them are blue. Can you point to the blue ones?

I don't think Peter will catch any of the butterflies do you? Perhaps this little rhyme will explain why.

Peter White

Peter White will never go right.
Do you know the reason why?
He follows his nose wherever he goes,
And that stands all awry.

Muffin Man

Have you seen the muffin man?
The muffin man, the muffin man.
Oh, have you seen the muffin man
Who lives down Drury Lane?

Oh yes, I've seen the muffin man,
The muffin man, the muffin man.
Oh yes, I've seen the muffin man,
Who lives down Drury Lane.

How many people are waiting for the
muffin man? Has he got enough muffins
for everybody? Count the number of
muffins he has balanced on his nose.

9 nine

10
ten

Higgledy, piggledy

Higgledy, piggledy, my black hen,
She lays eggs for gentlemen.
Gentlemen come every day
To see what my black hen doth lay.
Sometimes nine and sometimes ten,
Higgledy, piggledy, my black hen.

Can you see ten gentlemen in the queue?
One of them is very small!

There were ten in the bed

There were ten in the bed
And the little one said,
'Roll over, roll over!'
So they all rolled over
And one fell out.

There were nine in the bed
And the little one said,
'Roll over, roll over!'
So they all rolled over
And one fell out.

There were eight in the bed
And the little one said,
'Roll over, roll over!'
So they all rolled over
And one fell out.

There were seven in the bed
And the little one said,
'Roll over, roll over!'
So they all rolled over
And one fell out.

There were six in the bed
And the little one said,
'Roll over, roll over!'
So they all rolled over
And one fell out.

There were five in the bed
And the little one said,
'Roll over, roll over!'
So they all rolled over
And one fell out.

There were four in the bed
And the little one said,
'Roll over, roll over!'
So they all rolled over
And one fell out.

There were three in the bed
And the little one said,
'Roll over, roll over!'
So they all rolled over
And one fell out.

There were two in the bed,
And the little one said,
'Roll over, roll over!'
So they all rolled over
And one fell out.

There was one in the bed
And the little one said,
'Roll over, roll over!'
So he rolled over,
And he fell out.

There was no one in the bed,
So no one said,
'Roll over, roll over!'

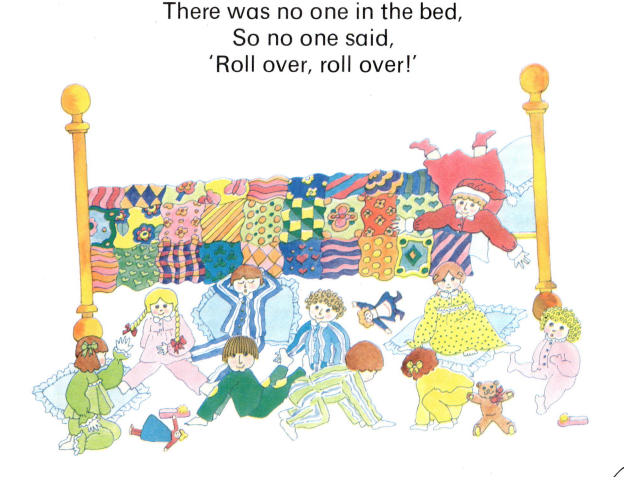

11 eleven

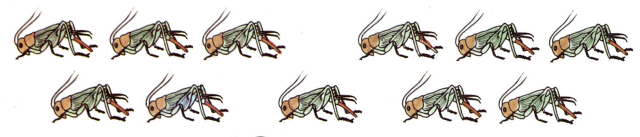

12 twelve

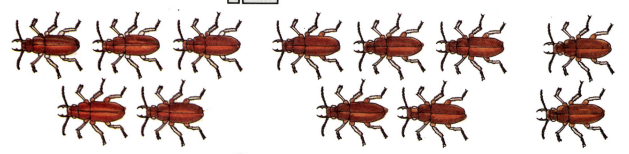

13 thirteen

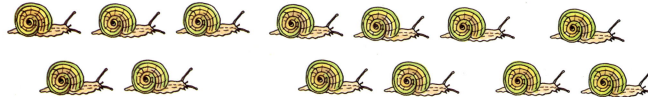

14 fourteen

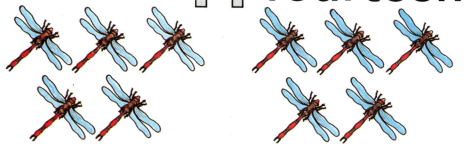

15 fifteen

16 sixteen

17 seventeen

18 eighteen

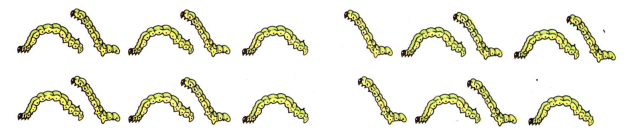

19 nineteen

20 twenty

How many cakes have blue icing?
How many cakes have pink icing?
How many cherries can you see?
How many cakes are there left for tea?

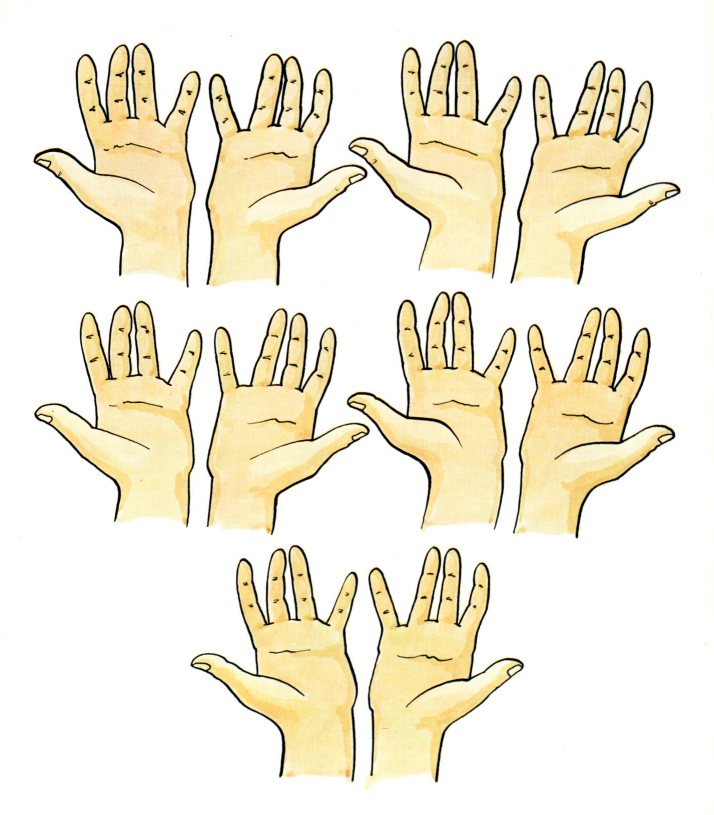

How many fingers on one hand?
How many fingers on two hands?
How many thumbs on two hands?
How many thumbs in the picture?

Pairs

Have you got a pair of shoes?
Have you got a pair of socks?
Have you got a pair of gloves?
How many shoes make up one pair?
Do the shoes have to match to make a pair?

How many brown shoes can you see in the picture? How many pairs of brown shoes can you see? Count all the shoes in the picture. How many are there? How many pairs are there?

Can you match the circus performers to their
props? The ring-master needs his hat. The
clown wants the balloons. The seal needs the
ball to balance on his nose. The strongman
needs the weights and the juggler his clubs.

The toyshop window

On Saturday Jamie and Jill went shopping with Mummy and Daddy. They stopped to look in the toyshop window.

'Look at all the toy cars!' shouted Jamie.

'How many cars can you see?' asked Daddy.

Can you help Jamie to count all the toy cars in the window?

Jill was looking at the teddy bears. 'I can see five bears, Daddy,' she said.

'There are five dolls too,' said Daddy. 'How many dolls and teddy bears are there altogether?' he asked.

Can you help Jill to count the dolls and the teddy bears? There are five dolls and five teddy bears. That makes ten altogether.

Jamie and Jill were enjoying this counting game so much that Mummy asked them some more questions. Jamie and Jill got all the answers right. Can you?

How many toys in the window can you use to make music?
How many soldiers can you see?
How many green cars are in the toyshop?
How many toys can you see altogether?

Cutting up cakes!

On Monday Mrs Bun the Baker made three cakes. The first cake she covered in soft pink icing. The next cake she covered in thick yellow icing, and the last cake she covered in lovely brown chocolate icing.

On Tuesday Mrs Jones came into the baker's shop with her two children. 'Please can I have that lovely yellow cake,' she said. 'Tony and Sarah have been helping me to dig the garden and I haven't had time to make any tea.'

When they got home, Mrs Jones cut the cake straight down the middle. 'That's half for you, Sarah,' she said. 'And Tony can have the other half. I shan't eat any because cake makes me fat!'

So Sarah and Tony had half the cake each.

On Wednesday Mr Robinson came into the baker's shop. 'Please can I have that pink cake,' he said. 'I will take it home as a surprise for my wife and my two children.'

When he got home Mr Robinson cut the pink cake into four equal pieces. 'That's one piece for you, my dear,' he said to his wife. 'One piece for Jack, one

piece for Tracey, and one piece for me.' So Mr and Mrs Robinson and Jack and Tracey had one quarter of the cake each.

On Thursday Angela ran to the baker's shop after school. 'It's my birthday today,' she told Mrs Bun. 'Five of my friends are coming to tea and Mummy says we can have chocolate cake!'

So Angela took the chocolate cake home and put it in the middle of the table until it was time for tea.

When everybody was sitting around the tea table Angela's Mummy cut the chocolate cake. First she cut it in half. Then she cut it in quarters. Then she cut each quarter in half again.

'Eight equal pieces of cake,' said Angela's Mummy. 'One piece of cake for each of Angela's five friends, one piece for Angela, one piece for Daddy and one piece for me. We're each going to eat an eighth of this delicious chocolate cake.'

Beetle

You will need
A grown-up to help explain how to play
Paper
Pencils
A dice

This is an exciting dice game which will help children to learn and remember numbers. Each player needs a pencil and a piece of paper. The game can be played with just two people or with a large group. The more people playing — the more fun it is!

How to play
Take it in turns to throw the dice. You need a six to start. As soon as one player has thrown a six then he can start by drawing a beetle body. On his next turn he must try and throw a five. You are only allowed to throw the dice once each time you have a turn so you have to keep on trying.

Remember — when you have thrown a six you can draw a beetle body. When you have thrown a five you can draw a beetle head. When you have thrown a four you can put on two front legs. When you have thrown a three you can put on the four back legs. A two means you can add the eyes and a one means you can complete your beetle with two antennae!

The first one to finish their beetle is the winner.

A game of pairs

You will need
A grown-up to help explain how to play
Pack of cards

Here is another game which will help children to learn numbers. It is a memory test too!

How to play
The rules are very simple. All you have to do is lay out a pack of cards face down on a large table or on the floor. There should be plenty of space between all the cards and they can be at a variety of angles.

The aim is for each player to find pairs of cards. The player who collects the most pairs is the winner.

The first player starts by picking up any two cards. If they are a pair — two sevens for example or two kings — then she puts them on one side and has another go. If the two cards she picks up this time are not a pair then she turns them face down again and someone else has a turn. Each player's turn continues for as long as she turns up pairs.

As the game goes on, anyone with a good memory should be able to remember where certain cards are. This will help them to make pairs. The winner is the one who has most pairs in their pile when all the cards are gone.

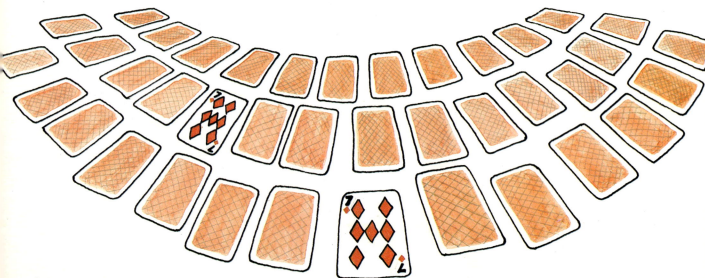

Shapes

After looking through this section and talking about the pictures, children will be interested in seeing the shapes they have learnt about repeated in objects all around them. Point out that the shapes can appear as tiny objects or as enormous ones. A postage stamp, for example, is a rectangle; so is a door. The wheels on a toy car are round; so are the wheels on a lorry.

Try to find some different shaped objects and get the child to draw round them. If you have time, cut out cardboard shapes, for the child to colour, and hang them up on pieces of string.

Square □

This window is square. The four windowpanes are square too. How many square things can you see around you?

Rectangle ▭

Doors are usually rectangular. If you look carefully you will see that the letter-box in the door is rectangular too. What is the shape of this book?

Paper aeroplane

You can make a paper aeroplane using a rectangular piece of paper. Ask a grown-up to help if you cannot manage on your own.

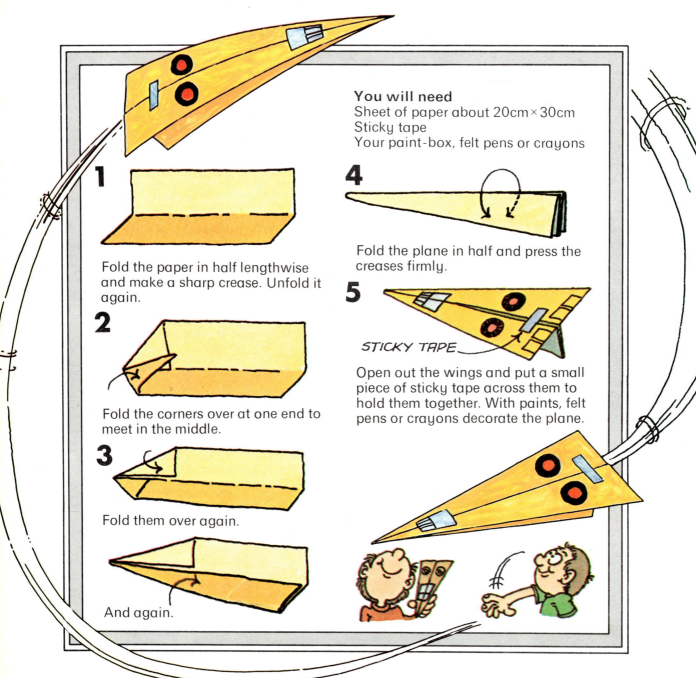

You will need
Sheet of paper about 20cm × 30cm
Sticky tape
Your paint-box, felt pens or crayons

1
Fold the paper in half lengthwise and make a sharp crease. Unfold it again.

2
Fold the corners over at one end to meet in the middle.

3
Fold them over again.

And again.

4
Fold the plane in half and press the creases firmly.

5
STICKY TAPE

Open out the wings and put a small piece of sticky tape across them to hold them together. With paints, felt pens or crayons decorate the plane.

Now it is ready to fly. Get your friends to make planes too and see whose plane will fly the furthest.

Circle ○

Circles are round like this little boy's hoop. Do you ever play games where you have to dance round and round in a circle? 'Ring-a-ring o'roses' is a game like that.

Ring-a-ring o'roses,
A pocket full of posies,

A-tishoo! A-tishoo!
We all fall down.

Circle mobile

Here is a mobile you can make using a circle of card and lots of other shapes. You will need a grown-up to help you make the mobile.

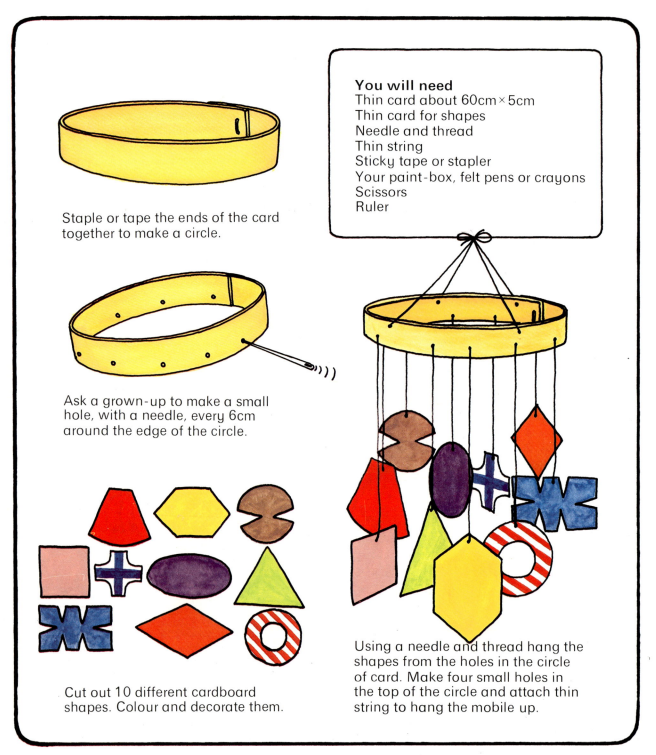

Staple or tape the ends of the card together to make a circle.

You will need
Thin card about 60cm × 5cm
Thin card for shapes
Needle and thread
Thin string
Sticky tape or stapler
Your paint-box, felt pens or crayons
Scissors
Ruler

Ask a grown-up to make a small hole, with a needle, every 6cm around the edge of the circle.

Cut out 10 different cardboard shapes. Colour and decorate them.

Using a needle and thread hang the shapes from the holes in the circle of card. Make four small holes in the top of the circle and attach thin string to hang the mobile up.

Snowflakes from circles

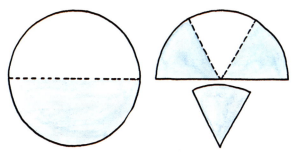

You will need
A grown-up to help
Sheet of plain paper
Scissors
Pencil
Saucer or plate

Lay a saucer or small plate on the paper and draw round it. Cut out the circle of paper. Fold it in half and then into a cone shape.

Cut the pointed top off the cone shape and cut different shaped notches in the sides and bottom of the cone. Open out the paper and you have your snowflake.

Snowflakes can be stuck on to windows for a Christmas decoration or use them as doilies on plates to make your party table look pretty.

Oval

Eggs have an oval shape. What colour are these eggs? Did you have an egg for breakfast today?

Oval mask

Make a mask! If you can't cut out an oval of card on your own, ask a grown-up to help you. But make sure you decorate the mask all by yourself. Are you going to make a monster face or a pretty face?

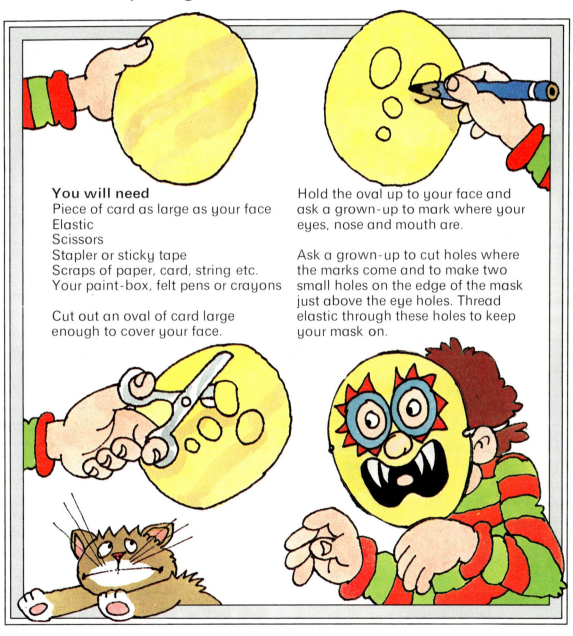

You will need
Piece of card as large as your face
Elastic
Scissors
Stapler or sticky tape
Scraps of paper, card, string etc.
Your paint-box, felt pens or crayons

Cut out an oval of card large enough to cover your face.

Hold the oval up to your face and ask a grown-up to mark where your eyes, nose and mouth are.

Ask a grown-up to cut holes where the marks come and to make two small holes on the edge of the mask just above the eye holes. Thread elastic through these holes to keep your mask on.

Now you can decorate your mask. Don't forget you can stick on hair and ears!

Triangle △

The sails on this boat are triangle-shaped.
What colour are the sails? What colour is the
boat?

Robin's boat

Robin had a boat with two sails. The sails were triangle-shaped. One sail was red and the other was yellow. The boat was bright blue.

Robin sailed his boat on the pond in the park near his house. There was a little sailor doll sitting in the cabin. Robin pretended the doll was a brave yachtsman who was sailing all round the world on his own.

Robin's friend Helen had a boat with square sails. Sometimes Robin and Helen went to the park together. Then they had a race to see whose boat could cross the pond first. Helen's boat usually won but her boat had three sails. Robin's boat only had two sails. Some children in the park had boats with engines. These boats went very fast. Robin didn't mind though. He liked his yacht best.

One day Robin went to the seaside with his Uncle and Aunt. He took along his boat. He wanted to sail it on the sea.

'Be very careful,' said Aunty Margaret. 'The sea is not like the pond in the park at home. Your boat may get blown out into deep water!'

But Robin didn't listen. He couldn't wait to put the boat into the waves. He gave it a push and the yacht skimmed away. The wind puffed out the sails. Before long the little boat was far out at sea.

Robin's Aunt and Uncle thought he would be very upset, but not a bit of it. Robin was very pleased. He knew his boat was off on its way around the world!

So if you see a little boat with red and yellow triangle-shaped sails, give it a wave. It probably belongs to Robin.

Diamond ◇

Look at the children flying their kites. The kites
are diamond-shaped. Have you got a kite?
What shape is your kite?

What do you think has happened to the yellow kite? It looks as if he has got all caught up in a blackberry bush. Do you think the mouse will try to help the kite get free? If the mouse does help the kite to get free perhaps the kite will give him a ride across the sky! Would you like to fly across the sky on a giant kite?

Shape quiz

How many triangles can you see?
Can you see a diamond shape?
Which is the biggest square in the picture?
Where is the oval shape?
How many rectangles can you see?
Which is the smallest circle in the picture?

Spiral

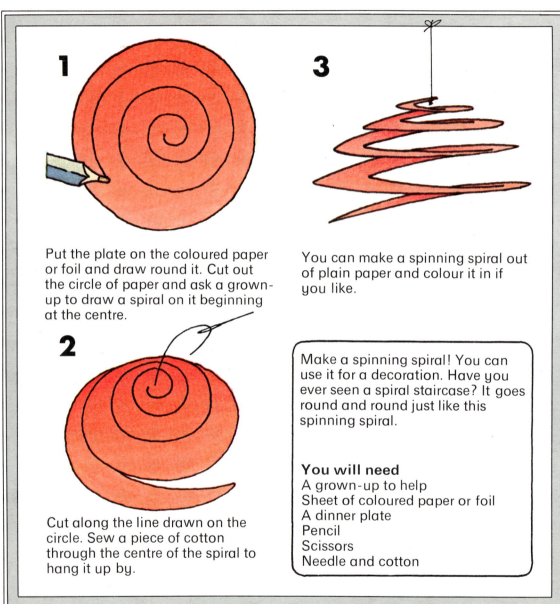

1

Put the plate on the coloured paper or foil and draw round it. Cut out the circle of paper and ask a grown-up to draw a spiral on it beginning at the centre.

2

Cut along the line drawn on the circle. Sew a piece of cotton through the centre of the spiral to hang it up by.

3

You can make a spinning spiral out of plain paper and colour it in if you like.

Make a spinning spiral! You can use it for a decoration. Have you ever seen a spiral staircase? It goes round and round just like this spinning spiral.

You will need
A grown-up to help
Sheet of coloured paper or foil
A dinner plate
Pencil
Scissors
Needle and cotton

Learning every day

Young children are learning all the time and you can greatly aid and encourage this process. If you are looking after a young child talk to them as much as possible. Name clothes as you put them on. Name parts of the body as you wash them! Explain about the seasons as the weather changes.

For a child to recognize simple written words is a great achievement. Putting 'labels' on a few everyday objects can help. Don't label more than four objects per room and print the labels. Never use capital letters. Once the child knows a word the label can be stuck in a scrapbook with a picture of the object beside it. Encourage the child to draw the picture or find one in an old magazine for them to cut out.

Parts of the body

Each part of your body has a name. Can you name all the parts of your body?

You have two eyes, two ears, a nose and a mouth. What colour are your eyes?

Are your teeth sparkling white? You must clean them every morning and every night.

How many toes have you got? How many fingers?

Make your body work!
Jump up and down.
Sit on the floor.
Clap your hands.
Hop on one foot.
Run on the spot.
Walk backwards.
Wriggle your toes.
Can you do all these things?

Are you tired now? See if you can keep very, very still. Don't speak! You mustn't even move your mouth. How long can you stay absolutely still without moving or speaking? Have you ever tried talking without opening your mouth? Try it! It is very hard to do.

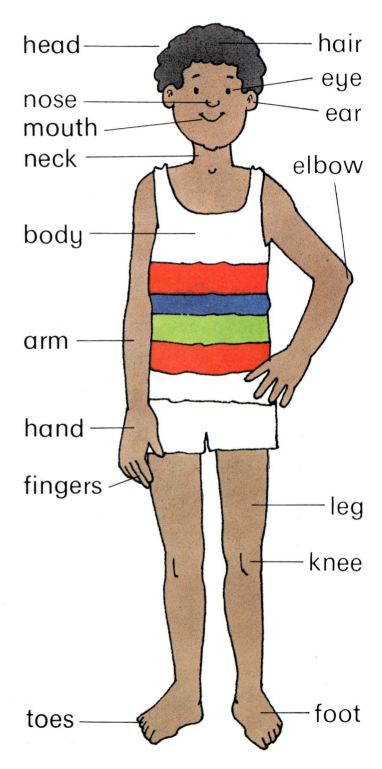

head — hair
nose — eye
mouth — ear
neck
elbow
body
arm
hand
fingers — leg
— knee
toes — foot

Clothes

dress	handkerchief	knickers	coat
pants	jersey	raincoat	scarf
shirt and tie	shorts	skirt	socks
trousers	shoes	vest	slippers

Here are pictures of some clothes. Do your clothes look like this? Can you name all the pictures?

Match the bodies and legs

Can you match the bodies and legs so that the children are wearing the right clothes?

One of the boys is wearing orange dungarees.
What colour is his hair?
One of the girls is wearing a green dress.
What colour are her hair ribbons?

One of the boys has a brown jersey.
What colour are his shoes?
One of the girls has a blue dress.
What colour is her blouse?

Day

It is daytime. The sun is shining and the children are playing on the beach. Some people are swimming in the sea.

Night

It is night-time. The children are all in bed.
Now it is dark the coloured lights have been
switched on. They look pretty don't they?

wardrobe

lamp

mirror

comb

shoes

stool

blanket

bed

dressing-gown

rug

slippers

trousers

socks

Lisa's bedroom

Look at Lisa tucked up in bed asleep. What colour are her pyjamas?

Does your bedroom look like this? Lisa's bedroom is very tidy. Is your bedroom as tidy as hers?

Can you see the moon and stars shining outside Lisa's window? Next time you are still awake when it is dark look up in the sky and see if you can see the moon. The moon shines at night. What shines during the day?

Lisa is having a dream. She is dreaming that tomorrow is Saturday and that she is going to tea with her friend Andrew.

Saturday is Lisa's favourite day but she likes Sunday too. On Sunday Lisa often goes to tea with her Grandma. On Monday, Tuesday, Wednesday, Thursday and Friday Lisa goes to school. She likes school really!

Which day of the week do you like the best?

Solomon Grundy

Solomon Grundy,
Born on Monday,
Christened on Tuesday,
Married on Wednesday,
Took ill on Thursday,
Worse on Friday,
Died on Saturday,
Buried on Sunday.
This is the end
Of Solomon Grundy.

Months

January	February	March
April	May	June
July	August	September
October	November	December

There are twelve months in every year. Which is your favourite month? Lots of people like December because that is when Christmas comes. Which month is your birthday in?

Seven days make a week — Monday, Tuesday, Wednesday, Thursday, Friday, Saturday and Sunday. There are fifty-two weeks in a year. So fifty-two weeks make one year and twelve months make one year too. Here is a rhyme which will help you to remember how many days there are in each month.

Thirty days hath September,
April, June and November.
All the rest have thirty-one
Excepting February alone,
Which has twenty-eight days clear
And twenty-nine in each leap year!

Spring

Summer

The Seasons

Autumn

Winter

The weather

What sort of weather do you like? Do you like playing in the sun or do you prefer splashing about in the rain? Perhaps you like both. Windy days are fun too. Sometimes the wind is so strong that it blows you along the street!

Memory game

You will need
A grown-up to help
A tray
Pencils
Paper
Objects from around the house

How to play

Ask a grown-up to put about twelve small objects on a tray. Choose everyday things from around the house — a comb, an apple, a button, scissors and so on.

All the children playing are allowed to look at the tray for five minutes. Then the grown-up takes the tray away.

Now you must try to remember how many objects you saw. If you can't write down all the names, draw little pictures of the objects you remember seeing. The person who can remember most is the winner.

Subtraction

Here is another memory game. It is a good game to play when grown-ups want a rest! All they have to do is sit in a chair and watch you playing.

First of all everyone has a good look round the room and tries to remember everything that is there. Now the grown-up sends everyone out of the room and hides one object.

When all the children come back in, they have to guess which object is missing.

Can you be the first to guess?

Alphabet

An alphabet section is included in this book because words are made up of letters and children need to be able to discriminate between one letter and the next. In the early stages of learning it is wise *not* to introduce letter sounds. Simply call each letter by its name. The reason for this is obvious. The sound a letter makes often varies according to where it occurs in a word. For example, 'e' in pen makes quite a different sound from the 'e' in beautiful.

A good way of helping children to master the shape of words is to encourage them to cut pictures from magazines and stick them into their own scrapbook. This will eventually form an 'I-Spy' book of their own. The names of objects can be written underneath — but remember if you do this to print the word in lower case. Never use capital letters when writing words for children.

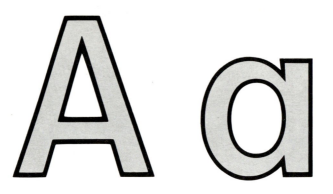

Amanda is an artist. She is painting an ark
and an arrow. What has she drawn up in the sky?

B b

Brian is riding his bicycle with a bell on it.
He is carrying his boots. What else is he carrying?

C c

Cathy is a cook and she has just baked a cake. Somebody is sitting in the cupboard watching Cathy. Who is it?

D d

Diana is digging a deep ditch while her dog eats his dinner. Can you see the flower in the picture? Do you know what it is called?

E e

Edward is going to eat eggs for breakfast.
There is one fried egg on the plate already.
What do you need if you are going to eat
boiled eggs?

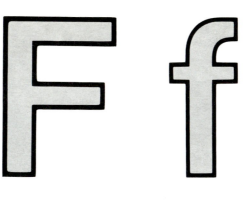

Frank is a farmer and he is carrying flowers
and fruit. What has Frank got to climb over?

G g

Grandma and Grandpa are sitting in the garden.
What colour is the grass?

H h

Harry is getting into the helicopter.
What is he wearing on his head?

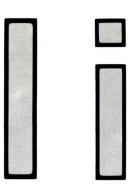

Isabel is writing an invitation. What is in the big bottle? When she has finished the invitation Isabel is going to iron some clothes.

J j

Jim the juggler is going to juggle with the things he is holding. In one hand he has a jug of jelly. What is he holding in the other hand?

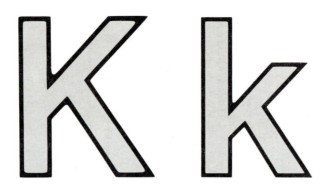

K k

Kevin is in the kitchen looking for his kitten.
There is a kettle on the table. What is the
kitten playing with under the table?

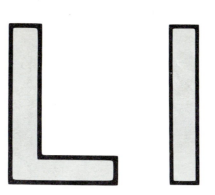

Louise is in the library looking for a letter she has lost. Where is the letter?

M m

Monty the magician has a mouse on one arm
and a monkey on the other. What is the
monkey holding?

N n

Nicola has been shopping. She has bought some nails and some nuts. What else has she bought?

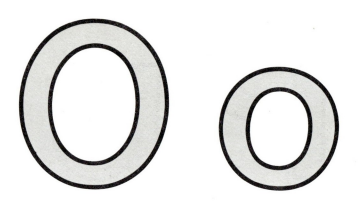

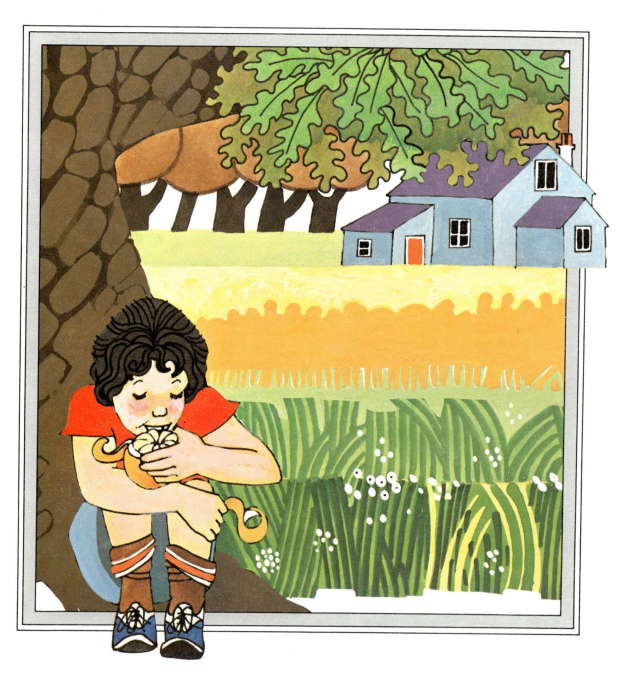

Oliver is sitting under an old oak tree.
What is he eating?

Patrick is taking his pig and his pony to the pond. What colour is the pig?

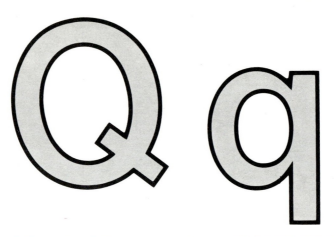

Queenie is in bed reading a quiz. The quiz has lots of questions. What sort of cover does Queenie have on her bed?

R r

Rosie is sitting on a rock by the river. She has a red ribbon in her hair. What can you see in the sky?

S s

Sam the sailor is on his ship.
Who is sitting on Sam's shoulder?

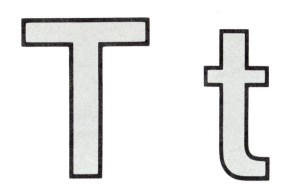

T t

Ted has been shopping. He has bought a tambourine and a trombone. What else has he bought?

U u

Una is very untidy. Her shoelace is undone
and her book is upside down. What is behind
her chair?

V v

Vicky is going to drive her van into the village.
What is she putting into the van?

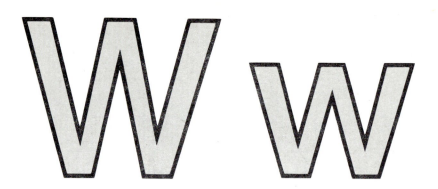

William is washing his face. He has taken off his watch so it won't get wet. Where is his watch?

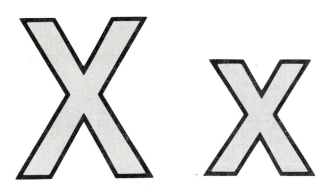

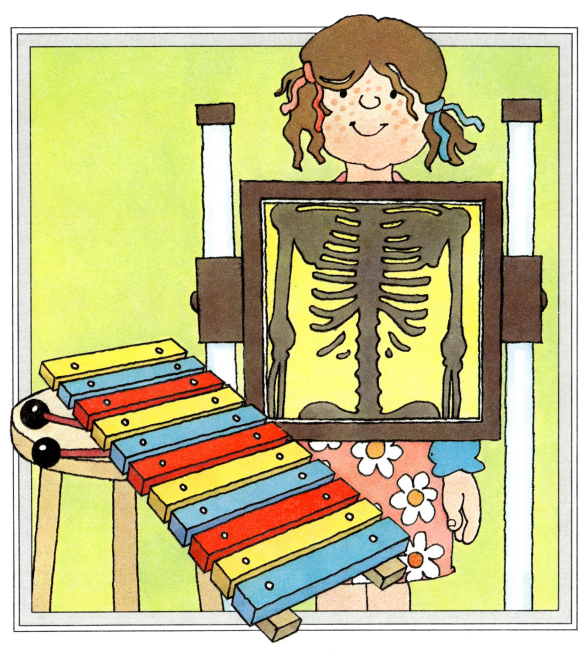

Xenia is in hospital having an X-ray. She has brought one of her toys with her. Do you know what it is?

Y y

Yvonne and Yolande are eating yogurt. What colour is the flower in the vase behind them?

Z z

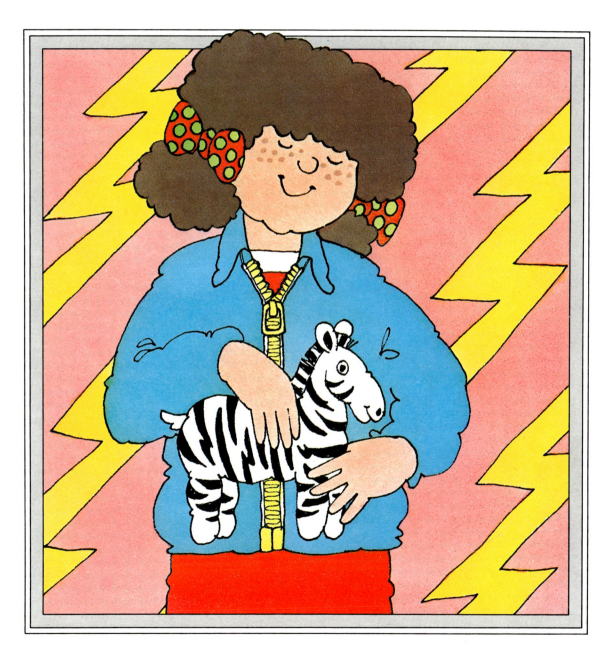

Zoë has got a big zip down the front of her jacket. She is playing with one of her favourite toys. What is it?

page 102
e
some eggcups

page 103
f
a fence

page 104
g
green

page 105
h
a helmet

page 111
n
a newspaper

page 112
o
an orange

page 113
p
pink

page 114
q
a quilt

page 115
r
a rainbow

page 120
w
by the window

page 121
x
a xylophone

page 122
y
yellow

page 123
z
a zebra